Talking With Your Child About

GOD'S STORY

Linda M. Harle-Mould
Hope Douglas J. Harle-Mould

A Growing Together Series Book

United Church Press   •   Cleveland, Ohio

Rev. Linda M. Harle-Mould, a mother, wife, and actress, serves on the Board of Directors of the United Church Board for Homeland Ministries.

Rev. Hope Douglas J. Harle-Mould serves as associate pastor of the Dublin Community United Church of Christ, Dublin, Ohio.

Writers: Linda M. Harle-Mould and Hope Douglas J. Harle-Mould
Editor: Carol A. Wehrheim
Project Supervisor: Patricia J. Goldberg

United Church Press
Cleveland, Ohio 44155

Cover logo by Andrew Hardin

Printed in the United States of America
The paper used in this publication is acid free and meets the minimum requirements of American National Standard for Information Sciences-Permanence of Paper for Printed Library Materials, ANSI Z39.48-1984

98   97   96   95   94   93   5   4   3   2   1

Library of Congress Cataloging-in-Publication Data

Harle-Mould, Linda M. (Linda Marie) 1952-
        Talking with your child about God's story / Linda M. Harle-Mould, Hope Douglas J. Harle-Mould.
        p. cm. — (A Growing together series book)
        Includes bibliographical references.
        ISBN 0-8298-0955-4 (alk. paper)
        1. Children—Religious life. 2. Christian education of children.
I. Harle-Mould, Hope Douglas J. (Hope Douglas John), 1953-
II. Title. III. Series.
BV4571.2H37   1993
248.8'45—dc20
                                                        92-41972
                                                            CIP

In the beginning was the Story—
not a single syllable, one word with one meaning,
but the beginning of action moving into history.

It is a Story full of plots, characters, adventures.
In an early morning garden, on a leaky zoo boat,
around a burning bush, a dusty manger,
a splintered cross, a fishfry at sunrise,
it is the one Story which invites
each one's own story into being, into telling.

Such a simple Story, but so difficult to hear.
Abraham laughed. Jonah scoffed.
Peter forgot it. Jesus repeated it
in as many ways as he could
until he finally had to become it.
A simple Story of love.[1]

THE WONDER OF STORYTELLING

Gathered together around a campfire are mothers, fathers, and children. The wind whispers quietly and the stars twinkle. A small child raises a simple question: "Where did the stars come from?" After a pause, a parent answers: "In the beginning, God . . ."

The scene, the questions, and the answers have followed the same pattern from the campfires of ancient Israel to the RVs of modern America. Where did this come from? Why are we here? Where are we going? These questions are as instinctive to human nature as eating and sleeping. The answers, too, are instinctively known and point to someone or something greater than ourselves as the source, the meaning, the goal. And the natural means for conveying these mysteries is the telling of stories.

We learn about our families through stories told about family members. "Daddy, how did you meet Mama?" "Did great-great-grandpa really drive a stagecoach?" "Were grandma's parents really slaves?" "Our family was on the Trail of Tears?" The stories our memories gather give us a sense of who we are, of *whose* we are.

The Bible is the unified memory of the family of God. Its stories about our ancestors in faith give us a sense of our place in all of history, a sense of our heritage, our home. We need to tell the Bible's stories in the same way that we tell stories about our family members. If it's all right to laugh about Uncle Karl's first attempts at speaking English, then it's all right to chuckle about Moses saying that he can't really speak in public well enough to be God's voice. If we shed a tear over the tragic death of a family member, we might well do the same upon hearing the story of the death of Absalom, beloved son of David. If we are puzzled by the estrangements among our relatives, we can feel that same puzzlement as we hear about Cain and Abel or about Martha and Mary.

The Bible is not a book to be held in awe. Reverence, yes—just as we revere the stories of our families—but awe, no. Awe holds us apart from the scripture. To become tellers of the Word, we need to reclaim the Bible as our own story, our own history—a collection of tales that we have the right to tell.

"Mama, how did you meet Daddy?" "Well, in the beginning . . ." "Mama, where did the world come from?" "Well, in the beginning . . ." When parent and child come together, one to tell and one to hear a story, three things of wonder occur. First, the edges of the room seem to gradually become blanketed by fog as word after word of the story is heard—until finally the familiar surroundings are entirely shrouded. Then, as the story unfolds, the fog lifts to reveal a bright, new landscape beckoning them to enter and explore. "Everything old has passed away; see, everything has become new" (2 Corinthians 5:17).

Second, to tell a story to your children is to lead them beyond the rules, "correct" answers, and boundary lines of their daily experience. Stories allow them to glimpse the possibilities for thinking and living they have never dreamed.

And third, storytelling gives you as adult a portal back to the world of childhood, allowing you to become your child's peer, enabling you to become captivated, as in the past, by the power and the truth in the simplicity of story.

When the story you tell is from scripture, you are giving your child an additional wonder: the gift of a true story. Even the stories in the Bible that were composed as works of fiction (Ruth, Job, or Jonah) or the stories composed as explanations of truth (Creation or the Garden of Eden) are true stories in the deepest sense. They illuminate life. They are stories to live by.

A true story must either help us to see the world as it is or show what it can become. Most television stories do neither. . . . True stories lift our vision for the future or enable us to create a world that is more caring and humane. . . . The true story has an impact on our lives, helping us understand our own stories. . . . As Elie Wiesel has suggested, true stories are meant to be transmitted: "To keep them to oneself is to betray them."[2]

THE WORD IS NOT THE WORDS

We often refer to the Bible as the Word of God, but this can be taken to an extreme. When people equate the words of the Bible with the Word of God, they end up creating a new divinity, a fourth member of the Trinity. The Word is not the words. What, then, is the Word of God? That's simple. The Word of God is Jesus, the Word Made Flesh.

The Word of God is a message. Throughout the history of Israel, God sought to speak this message through covenant and prophets and acts in history. But humanity was a difficult audience to reach. Ultimately, God chose to deliver the message in person. God showed up as a baby, to incarnate the message, so that we would not only hear the word but learn to live it.

But if Jesus Christ is the Word of God, what is the Bible? That's easy. The Bible is the story of the message. It is the central way we know the Word Made Flesh, the Word Incarnate. The Bible is a storybook. It contains an inspired story, the story of how God loved and prodded and shaped and abandoned and delivered and emboldened and nurtured and suffered with the children made in God's image.

The secret power of this storybook, however, is that it is a neverending story. As we read it, our story connects with God's story. The story of our life becomes enmeshed in the continuation of the story of God.

God uses this storybook to open us to the divine dimension. By being drawn to the story of God, our life story changes. We find glimpses of truth and sources of strength within the Bible's pages. Ancient tales come alive by affecting us today. Even God's failures in the past—prophets whose messages went unheeded—can become, through the retold story, hidden keys for us in the present as we face formidable conflicts and are given the insights we need to triumph.

To connect with God's story is to change the ending of our own story.

THE POWER OF STORIES TO EVOKE FAITH

> The message and method of Jesus were inevitably tied together. It was impossible for Jesus to communicate his dynamic message through abstract language. . . . The use of storytelling is not simply a matter of taste, but an issue of faith. . . . Story evokes a more powerful faith response than doctrine and concept.[3]

When you think back on sermons you've heard, what do you most remember? You probably don't remember many of the points of argumentation, but there's probably one thing you do recall: the illustrations.

Which is most likely to influence us in a lasting way: the part of Paul's letter to the Romans that states we are saved by grace through faith or the parable of Jesus in which a father runs to embrace his lost son–a son who made all the wrong choices–and throws a gala in honor of his return? Jesus' portrait of a God of extravagant love (the father in the parable) is a theological truth that grabs us in a way dogmas cannot.

As we begin to search for biblical stories to tell our children, we need to be open to the depth that exists in the simplest of stories. Many of the Bible's stories are rich lodes of meaning, and at different points in our lives we might unearth new insights from the same passage. Noah is a perfect example. Even the youngest children love Noah's story because of the big boat and all the animals. As children grow older they begin to understand the meaning of the rainbow, God's promise to us. Later they appreciate the rainbow as a covenant not only between God and the Jews but between people of ethnic groups all over the earth. And finally, as adults, we might see in the story something we never noticed before–the first tragedy that occurs after the flood: Noah becomes the first alcoholic.

Within the familiar biblical story are many depths to explore. In the old, old stories there are for us grown children many images and meanings awaiting discovery.

HOW TO TELL THE STORY

There are many ways to tell a Bible story. The guidelines here are just that—guidelines to help you tell the stories of the Bible to your child, not to transform you into a professional storyteller. You have your own style. Use it.

You can't tell a story you don't know. Read the Bible story you have chosen several times. Listen as you read it aloud to yourself. Read between the lines, imagining the action and feelings going on in the story. Get to know the characters and plot until the story becomes familiar.

Don't be afraid to fill in the blanks to make a Bible story more interesting and memorable for your child. Do not, however, create alternative facts. If the most important facts of the story are not yet in your memory bank, write them down.

Don't read it—tell it! Practice telling the story. When we are with friends and tell them about something funny that once happened to us, chances are we have told that story before. Our best stories are those we have polished through retelling, through simplifying them until each phrase helps build toward the story's climax. The best Bible stories are those we retell in our own words, in our own way.

Remember the bare essentials. Within each story are deeper truths that are more important than all the details. Some of the details help us remember the story. Others help us enjoy the story. But many of the details that we tend to forget are not really crucial. The power of the story is still present in the essentials we recall. If we tell a story with love and enthusiasm, our children will never know what we have forgotten to include—at least until they are old enough to read it for themselves!

Tell the story eye-to-eye. Whenever you tell your children a story, look at them. The eye is the window to the soul. Your mouth may tell your children the line of a story, but its deepest meanings will be revealed only by what they see sparkling in your eyes.

Develop verbal and facial expressions. Let the stories of scripture be entertainment and the education will take care of itself. Draw out the mystery stories to their Alfred Hitchcock best. Let the love stories be worthy of Romeo and Juliet. Let the tragedies make the tears flow. The Bible tells us that we are to be fools for Christ's sake. Storytelling is one of the most important places to let that foolishness show. Exaggerate. Play different parts. Go ahead–be a child yourself.

For God's sake, laugh. We mean that quite literally. Our God has a marvelous sense of humor, and if we look at the stories of the Bible through open, childlike eyes, we will see many pages of scripture punctuated by the chuckles of God. For example, at the wedding feast in Cana (John 2:1-12), can you picture the expression on Jesus' face when his mother tries to talk him into doing something he doesn't want to do? You know what that looks like, that "Mother, please" look.

Believe the story. If you say the words without expressing them, you will be unbelievable. Feel what you are saying and your children will sense your sincerity.

If you don't care about a story, don't tell it. Your children will see through the attempt and discount the story. In our family, Hope tells some stories and Linda tells others. Each of us shares the stories that we enjoy or appreciate most. It is better that way— more honest, more joyful–for both parent and child.

Don't force the story to have a moral. Tell the story for its own sake. Let it work its own magic. For example, in the parable of the prodigal son (Luke 15:11-32), we as parents may want to give special emphasis to the father's climactic words: "For this son of mine was dead but is alive again; he was lost

12

and is found!" That's good, but also give equal emphasis to other parts of the story; depending on their ages, your children will hear what they need.

As you read children's Bibles or Bible storybooks, be alert for authors who have written the stories to include a moral for the children. A good story—and the Bible is full of them—presents truths without that device.

Relax and enjoy it. Have fun telling the story. Pretend it happened to you. Use different voices and different body postures. The more fun the story is for you, the more fun it will be for your child.

Learn from other storytellers. Your public library probably has recordings of fables and tales narrated by professional actors. Listen to them. Pay attention to the ways professionals use their voices and how they frame a story. Go and do likewise!

From time to time, show your children where the story you are telling is found in the Bible. Although the Word of God is not tied to the printed pages, your child will gain an appreciation for this book that is so important to the church only if others show their appreciation for it.

Finding the Stories to Tell

So far we have discussed the importance of becoming a parent who is a teller of the Word, God's Word. But you may be wondering, How do I get started? Where do I find stories that my children can enjoy now and also take with them as they grow?

You probably know more stories from the Bible than you think you do. Think for a moment. What stories from the Old Testament or Hebrew Scriptures are your favorites? Do you remember the stories of Creation, Adam and Eve, and Abraham's near-sacrifice of his son Isaac? How about baby Moses found on the river in a basket, Moses and the burning bush, the crossing of the Red Sea, and the receiving of the

Ten Commandments? And what about David and Goliath, or Jonah in the belly of the great fish? How many others do you recall?

Some of these stories you may know well enough to tell in a simplified way at this very moment. Even if you have forgotten parts of a story, you may recall key scenes. (If you don't know any of these stories, stay with us and we'll show you where to find wonderful stories that both you and your children can enjoy.)

Now let's think about the New Testament. Imagine you came across a first-grade child who knew nothing about Jesus—who Jesus was or what Jesus did. What could you tell this youngster about the events surrounding Jesus' birth, or the Last Supper, Crucifixion, and Resurrection? Few of us have ever tried to tell the Jesus story in one sitting, but it would be a marvelous exercise. We would discover which parts of Jesus' teachings and ministry have made indelible imprints on our minds.

Let's go one step further. Imagine you were asked to tell the entire Jesus story from memory once a week for twelve weeks. Your first telling would probably be rough and disjointed, with some parts out of order and others forgotten. But as you told the story week after week, you would gradually increase the number of characters and events and make the action smoother, more detailed and dramatic.

You're probably saying, "Okay, so I have more biblical material in my head than I realized. Still, much of the Bible is unknown to me. How can I locate more of the Bible's greatest stories, especially stories to tell my children?" That's just what we want to discuss now.

Becoming a Reader of the Bible

The best way to learn more about the Bible is to read it. Simply pick it up and read some of the strange and delightful and surprising stories it holds.

Where do you start? Try this. Sit down one evening and read right through the Gospel of Mark. The shortest of the four Gospels, it has only sixteen chapters, a mere twenty-eight pages in most Bibles. Mark's Gospel is a down-to-earth, fast-moving portrait of Jesus. You will find many good stories and at the same time get a feel for the sweep of the entire Jesus story.

Your most important task as a student of scripture is to get a grasp of the entire theme and scope of the Bible, to get the big picture. Reading one gospel is not that difficult, but how do you get the big picture of the entire Old Testament—indeed, the entire Bible? A good way is to read a children's Bible storybook. Look in your church or public library, see the Resources section at the end of the book, or ask your pastor or church educator for suggestions. A children's Bible can provide you with a unified series of scriptures retold in simple, direct language. Reading the stories will quickly familiarize you with the key stories of the Old Testament and provide you with an overview.

Once you gain some familiarity with the Old Testament, you may become curious enough to read specific stories in your own Bible to discover what meanings and nuances await you as an adult listening to this story. To learn more about the continuing themes of the Bible and how it came to be, see *Talking With Your Child About the Bible*, another Growing Together book.

Finding Your Way Around the New Testament

A children's Bible can familiarize you with Bible stories, but it won't help you find them in your own Bible. To get a feel for how the Bible is organized, flip through the pages of one book and scan the headings of each section. Some Bibles list the titles of the more familiar stories at the top of the page—forcing you to hunt on that page for where the story begins and ends. Other Bibles, and many newer translations such as the Good News Bible or the New Revised Standard Version, have titles that describe the topic of the story or theme that follows. This feature makes it easier to page through any part of the Bible to locate subjects that spark your interest.

Using this method, turn to the New Testament. Flip through the Gospel of Luke, the third book of the New Testament. Look for stories that you might enjoy telling your children.

Here are some stories from Luke that we think children between the ages of three and seven might enjoy:

The Boy Jesus in the Temple (2:41-51)
Jesus Calls His First Disciples (5:1-11)
Jesus Calms a Storm (8:22-25)
Feeding of the Five Thousand (9:10-17)
Parable of the Lost Sheep (15:3-7)
Jesus Heals Ten Lepers (17:11-19)
Jesus Blesses Little Children (18:15-17)
Jesus and Zacchaeus (19:1-10)
The Widow's Offering (21:1-4)

Children ages eight to twelve can learn from and enjoy additional stories from Luke. The ones we found are:

Jesus Heals a Paralyzed Man (5:17-26)
Parable of the Samaritan (10:25-37)
Mary and Martha (10:38-42)
Parable of the Rich Fool (12:13-21)
Jesus Heals a Crippled Woman (13:10-17)
Parable of the Great Dinner (14:15-24)
Parable of the Lost Son (15:11-32)
Parable of Widow and Unjust Judge (18:1-8)
Parable of Pharisee and Tax Collector (18:9-14)
Jesus Heals a Blind Man (18:35-43)
Peter Denies Jesus (22:54-62)

You can use this same technique of looking through a particular book to locate other stories from the

Gospels of Matthew, Mark, and John. And don't forget the Acts of the Apostles, a tale of dangers, travels, and interesting personalities, the story of the church's birth and growth from Jerusalem to Rome.

Finding Your Way Around the Old Testament

When it comes to the thirty-nine books of the Old Testament, the leaf-through technique can be very time-consuming unless there is some way to narrow your search. And there is. The vast majority of the most memorable stories in the Old Testament are concentrated in just four books: Genesis, Exodus, 1 Samuel and 2 Samuel. (Another group of books worthy of mention is: Joshua, 1 Kings, 2 Kings, and Daniel.) Select one book to investigate, and read the subject titles of each section as you page through it. Before long you will find yourself drawn to reading a story that has grabbed your attention.

A few of the best stories for children ages three to seven from Genesis, Exodus, and 1 and 2 Samuel are:

The Second Creation Story (Genesis 2:4–25)
Noah, Ark, Flood, Dove and Rainbow (Genesis 6:11–22; 7:6–10; 8:1–19; 9:8–17)
Birth of Esau and Jacob (Genesis 25:19–28)
Birth and Youth of Moses (Exodus 2:1–10)
Crossing the Red Sea (Exodus 14:1–31)
God Calls the Boy Samuel (1 Samuel 3:1–21)
Shepherd Boy Chosen as King (1 Samuel 16:1–13)
David Plays Music for King (1 Samuel 16:14–23)
David's Friend Jonathan (1 Samuel 20:1–42)

There are many more stories appropriate for ages eight to twelve from these four books. Some interesting ones include:

Cain Murders Abel (Genesis 4:1–16)
Abram and Lot Separate (Genesis 13:5–12)

Jacob and Esau: Birthright, Blessing, Forgiven (Genesis 25:29–34; 27:1–40; 32:3–21; 33:1–11)

Jacob Wrestles with God (Genesis 32:24–32)

Joseph is Sold, Pharaoh's Dream, and Brothers Meet (Genesis 37:12–36; 41:1–36; 42:1–25)

Moses Flees, Burning Bush, Many Excuses (Exodus 2:11–22; 3:1–12; 4:10–17)

Bricks Without Straw (Exodus 5:1–23)

The Tenth Plague and the Exodus (Exodus 12:29–42)

Bread from Heaven (Exodus 16:1–31)

Golden Calf, Broken Tablets (Exodus 32:1–20)

Moses Makes New Tablets (Exodus 34:1–5, 27–28)

David Cares for Mephibosheth (2 Samuel 9:1–13)

The Prophet Nathan and David (2 Samuel 12:1–15)

Several Old Testament books were written intentionally as short stories. These include Ruth, that great story of devotion across racial and family lines; Esther, the story of a beautiful Jew who saves her people from a holocaust; and Jonah, perhaps the most entertaining story in the entire Old Testament, and one which is closest in spirit to the parables of Jesus. The first two of these are best told in condensed form, whereas Jonah can be read or told just as it is.

One way to familiarize young children with scriptural stories is to offer to read them two bedtime stories, one from the Bible and one from their usual storybooks.

For the Bible story, you may use a children's Bible with attractive illustrations or the Good News Bible with its wonderful line drawings. Have your child point to an illustration that looks interesting. Under the line drawings in the Good News Bible is the reference to show you where the depiction can be found. Or read one story each night from a children's Bible, pausing to repeat those stories your child particularly enjoys.

We used the pick-an-illustration style with our daughter, who was fascinated with the picture of the paralyzed man being lowered by his friends through the roof to Jesus (Luke 5:17–26). Many evenings, she asked to hear that story first.

As you begin telling the stories, your children may start to ask you religious questions when you least expect them and when you have the least time to give a thoughtful answer. When that happens, do your best to offer a sincere response, even if that response is "I don't know. I've wondered about that, too." Ask your children what made them think of particular questions. Such questions don't appear out of thin air. But don't forget those questions! Take them seriously and follow them through. If you feel your answer is inadequate, that's okay. Feel free to bring up their question again after you have had some time to think it through.

Ask your pastor or church educator to help you find biblical stories that address particular questions. Don't look for the one and only answer. Look for stories that your children can grow into and up with, stories that will help them find their own answers.

Are you still feeling uneasy about telling Bible stories to your child? Remember, faith is not so much taught as caught, especially with children. The primary mode of children's learning is experiential. According to theories of faith development, a child first develops affiliative faith, faith that is caught as they are around it. Children absorb information like sponges. They learn best about God, life's purpose, and the Bible by means of osmosis. The home is their classroom, and you are the teacher.

As you live the Bible, the Bible will begin to live for your children. You may feel incapable of exemplifying the Bible. Don't worry–your children know perfectly well that you are no saint. But they will silently respect those things you hold highest and dearest. They will have some attraction to those things where your sincerity of conviction shines through, where they can see you are trying to learn and grow. If they catch you reading the Bible or looking up something in it, they may become intrigued themselves.

The object of being a teller of the Word is not to have

a verse to quote at children—as if that could ever be a helpful way of conveying God's message. No, the object is to open children to God's will, to the Realm of God, and to God's presence by means of stories from the Word.

When the Word of God isn't a Story

If we begin to make too many direct references to the Bible, our children are likely to rebel and turn off altogether. This often happens as children approach their pre-adolescent years. What do we do then? That's simple: don't let them know your words are from the Bible.

Sharing a thought from the Bible, such as the definition of love (1 Corinthians 13:4–7), is more important than mentioning where it is found. The point is to bring biblical images, phrases, and thinking into the everyday world of our children. Eventually, your children may discover where some of your words of wisdom can be found. They may hear them in worship, read them in classical literature, or stumble across them in the Bible and say, "Aha!" Or they may never know—it doesn't matter. The words of the Bible have escaped from the covers of the book and into your child's world.

When Hope was growing up, many times he heard his grandmother's assurance, "The Lord will provide." She usually said it when the family really needed to hear such words, during times of insecurity and crisis. When Grandma said these words, the family believed her because she had earned the right to say them. She believed those words right through the Great Depression. In the decades to follow, she lived those words as both an active member of her church and as a caring neighbor whose life revolved around helping those less fortunate than herself.

Grandma had passed on a biblical truth, although she never told the family that she was giving them a biblical message. (Read the story in Genesis 22:1–19.) What was more important than where her message came from was the fact that she had passed on to Hope a resource for living that he could rely on for years to come. Many times as an adult, when times were hardest, Hope remembered this saying.

Over the years, both of us have shared those words with others in times of need. They have never failed to help.

A BOOK OF WONDER

In Miss Margaret's class for young children at Grace United Church of Christ in Frederick, Maryland, the children participated in a simple ritual each Sunday: ringing the bell, looking at a picture of Jesus, thanking God for things important to them, and saying the Lord's Prayer. They did one other thing as well. They passed the classroom Bible around the circle. Each child had a chance to touch it and see it up close. It was the heaviest and thickest book that most of the children had encountered in their young lives, but they were not too young to learn what that book teaches: "Jesus loves me, this I know, for the Bible tells me so."

Hope remembers how much it meant to him to receive his first Bible. He was seven, it was Christmas, and the Bible was a gift from his mom and dad. To own his own Bible—which was a book he knew meant much to his parents, which he knew contained stories of Jesus, which he sensed was a clue to getting closer to the God he had always heard about—was a very special thing. In years to come, it would continue to be significant to Hope that he had received his first Bible not from his church (that happened a year later) but from his parents. His parents cared enough about him to buy this special book for him.

Young children have a heightened sense of the enchantment of life. Just from observing our attitudes as parents and our sense of reverence, children can catch the idea that there is something mysterious and unique about this book. That alone may be their earliest and most important lesson about the Bible.

We once heard the story of a one-year-old boy who had grown up in a home where God's name was mentioned on a regular basis. The mother was not religious in any extraordinary way, but she was sincere, and whenever God was spoken of, it was with reverence.

One evening, mother and son were outside when they noticed a beautiful full moon high in the starry sky. The toddler, carried in his mother's arms, reached one hand toward the bright lunar light and pronounced, "Moon!" Then the toddler suddenly drew his hand back and wrapped it around his mother's neck. He hugged his mother tightly, with his eyes all the while riveted to the glowing moon. Then he whispered one word: "God."

He was right. That full moon was something remarkably new, something wonder-filled, something of glorious beauty. That little boy connected what he was experiencing with the way his mother had always spoken of God—an experience of alleluia.

The words of the Bible become sacred only to the degree that they are made to come alive for the next generation. It's up to you. Will you become a teller of the Word?

"In the beginning . . ."

NOTES

1. By Margie Brown and reprinted from *alive now!*, November/December 1981, 30. © 1981 by The Upper Room. Used by permission.
2. William R. White, *Stories for Telling: A Treasury for Christian Storytellers* (Minneapolis: Augsburg Publishing House, 1986), 11-12.
3. Ibid., 16.

RESOURCES

Parents as Storytellers

Anderson, Craig. *Talking With Your Child About the Bible.* Cleveland: United Church Press, 1992.

Boyer, Ernest, Jr. *Finding God at Home: Family Life as Spiritual Discipline.* San Francisco: Harper, 1988.

Furnish, Dorothy Jean. *Experiencing the Bible with Children.* Nashville: Abingdon Press, 1990.

Macguire, Jack. *Creative Storytelling: Choosing, Inventing, and Sharing Tales for Children.* New York: McGraw-Hill Co./The Philip Lief Group, Inc., 1985.

White, William R. *Stories for Telling: A Treasury for Christian Storytellers.* Minneapolis: Augsburg Publishing House, 1986.

Bible Stories for Children

The Children's Bible in 365 Stories. Batavia, Ill.: Lion Publishing, 1985.

A Few Who Dared to Trust God. New York: American Bible Society, 1990.

Good News Bible (The Bible in Today's English Version). New York: American Bible Society, 1976.

The Lion Story Bible. A series of fifty-two small books, each containing a single story from the Bible. Batavia, Ill.: Lion Publishing, 1984.

The New Revised Standard Version Children's Bible. Grand Rapids, Mich.: Zondervan, 1989.

Tomie dePaola's Book of Bible Stories. New York: G. P. Putnam's Sons/Zondervan, 1990.